E I

R. Gu

HERALDRY

Rosemary Manning

Illustrated by Janet Price

A. & C. BLACK LTD

LONDON

BLACK'S JUNIOR REFERENCE BOOKS

General Editor: R. J. Unstead

ISBN 0 7136 0108 6

FIRST PUBLISHED 1966
REPRINTED 1971

© 1966 A. AND C. BLACK LTD.

PUBLISHED BY A. AND C. BLACK LTD.
4, 5 AND 6 SOHO SQUARE, LONDON, W1V 6AD

MADE AND PRINTED IN GREAT BRITAIN BY
MORRISON AND GIBB LIMITED, LONDON AND EDINBURGH

Contents

ACKNOWLEDGMENTS

The author and publishers wish to thank the various persons and public bodies concerned who have kindly granted their permission for the reproduction of arms in this book. Grateful thanks are also extended to C W. Scott-Giles, O.B.E., and the Heraldry Society for permission to include extracts from "The Siege of Caerlaverock" on page 21, and to Barclays Bank Limited for the shield illustration on page 5.

Illustration 7 is from *Ancient Greek, Roman and Byzantine Costume* by Mary Houston and illustrations 2, 22, 34, 39 and 40 from *Medieval Costume in England and France* by the same author; illustrations 26 and 43 are from *England: The Medieval Scene* by R. J. Unstead.

5. *The arms of Oakley*

Here are their armorial bearings, as the artist imagines them.

The negro's head above the shield is the family *crest*. The guide book says that a large house was built hereabouts by a Sir James Oakley in 1610. He was a slave-trader in the last years of Queen Elizabeth the First's reign. Many Englishmen made money by carrying African slaves to the Spanish colonies in America, and later to the English settlements in states like Virginia. Perhaps Sir James Oakley acquired his negro's head crest after making a fortune out of slave-trading.

The oak leaves and acorns on his shield are a pun on the family name of Oakley. Puns are very common in heraldry, and arms of this type are called *canting arms*.

When a man's armorial bearings are displayed, with helmet and crest above the shield, and sometimes with a pair of figures on either side, they are called an *achievement*. The shield itself is often termed a *coat of arms*, because in the Middle Ages the devices upon it were embroidered upon the wearer's tunic, or surcoat, as well.

Here is a picture of a medieval knight wearing a surcoat. He is Sir Hugh Calveley. He fought in the Hundred Years War in the army of Edward, the Black Prince, and when he retired from soldiering, he was made Governor of the Channel Islands. He died in 1393, and is buried at Bunbury church, in Cheshire.

Sir Hugh is wearing a close-fitting, pointed helmet, called a bascinet, but there is another helmet lying beneath his head, as though it were his pillow. This is the "great helm" which went right over the top of his head, covering his face. It was worn in battle and at tournaments. Another type of great helm is shown in picture 21. On top of the helm is fixed the knight's crest, a calf's head. Three calves appear on his surcoat, so you can see that this is another canting or punning coat of arms.

6. *Sir Hugh Calveley*

7

Here is a list of the heraldic terms which you have now met:

ACHIEVEMENT the shield, with helmet and crest. If the shield has *supporters* on either side, as you will see in some of the pictures, these are also part of the achievement.

ARMORIAL BEARINGS the devices on the shield, called bearings because you carried or "bore" them.

CANTING ARMS devices which pun on the family name.

COAT OF ARMS really the heraldic surcoat, but generally used for the shield or the whole achievement.

CREST the object placed above the shield, usually resting on a twisted piece of cloth called a *torse*, or a *wreath of the colours*.

There are two other words which you need to know, as they will often appear in this book:

FIELD the background colour of the shield. This is always mentioned first when you describe a shield. The field of the Oakley and the Calveley arms is the same: white, or to give it its proper heraldic name, *argent*. Although the word "argent" is French for silver, the colour is always shown as white on a shield.

CHARGES the objects displayed on the shield, such as the oak leaves and calves.

Heraldry has a language of its own, mostly taken from French. The description of a coat of arms is called the *blazon*. At first, it may seem almost as difficult to read as a foreign language. All the same, I shall use it from time to time, and by the end of the book you will find that you can understand many of the commoner terms used in blazoning a coat of arms.

Sir Hugh's surcoat, in picture 6, has a shaded band across the waist. On his shield, this would be placed across the centre, a wide horizontal band called a *fess*. The *field* is white, the *fess* is red, and the calves are black. From the blazon, you can easily work out what the heraldic names for the colours are: *Argent, a fess gules between three calves sable.*

1. Looking for Shields

1. *The shield of Barclays Bank*

It is more than four hundred years since any British soldier went into battle with a shield on his arm, yet if you walk down the main street of any big town, you are almost certain to see two or three shields, carrying what are called *armorial bearings*.

Most of the well-known banks have branches in town centres, and each will have its shield. Barclays Bank, for instance, has an eagle, with black and gold feathers, red tongue and claws. You may see the shield of a building society, or the arms of your local Council, or the signboard of a public house bearing the name and arms of a family who were once important landowners in the district.

Why are shields used in this age of guns, aeroplanes and rockets? What do the patterns and objects displayed upon them stand for? What is the point of modern corporations such as the B.B.C. paying a fee to possess armorial bearings?

Societies and groups of many kinds, both among children and grown-ups, like to have a badge. Bodies such as town councils, banks and railways find it useful to mark their property with some emblem. The objects they choose may be as common as a castle or a crown, or as unusual as a bear's paw or a dolphin. The important thing is that they should be easily recognisable, like the eagle of Barclays Bank. If they are displayed upon a shield, they are not, strictly speaking, badges but armorial bearings.

These "marks of identity", whether they belong to kings or county councils, baronets or banks, are governed by rules of heraldry that are hundreds of years old. The rules grew up at a time when knights actually carried shields in war and in tournaments. They displayed upon them the animals, crosses, swords and other devices which they had chosen to distinguish them from other knights.

2. *A medieval knight*

5

3. The shield of the B.B.C.

Cities, counties, universities and many other bodies adopted armorial bearings as time went on. The objects on the shield often have a meaning connected with the person or corporation which uses them. It is obvious, for instance, why the globe and stars were chosen for the shield of the B.B.C.

Have you noticed the armorial bearings of your own school, or of your county or town council? If you can find out what they are, they may tell you something of the past history of the school and of the place where you live.

This book has been written to help you to understand the heraldry that you will see around you. It tells you something about the history that lies behind many badges and shields, and the way the rules of heraldry have developed.

2. Down the Street

Let us suppose that you live at Number Ten, Orchard Street, in a Midlands town. You do not know why it is called that. There isn't an orchard for miles. On the corner of your street stands a public house called the "Oakley Arms", with a coloured shield hanging outside it. When you go to the shops, you find yourself in Avenue Road, although there is not a tree in sight.

4. The "Oakley Arms"

Most big towns have grown up fairly recently. Houses and streets have been built on land that was once part of large estates owned by country gentlemen or noblemen, coming from families who may have lived there for centuries and played an interesting part in local or national history.

What about the Oakley family? Probably Orchard Street was once part of their estate. Fruit-trees really grew there, and the manor house may have stood nearby, approached through an avenue of trees where now your main shopping centre is built. Who were the Oakleys? A guide-book in the local public library would tell you.

3. Badges

A coat of arms is, in a way, a rather elaborate form of badge, and the wearing of devices on armour, on battle standards and spear pennons and at the mastheads of ships, is as old as war itself. The ancient Greeks, for instance, decorated their round shields with figures of lions, wild boar, fish, snakes and other emblems. You may belong to some society yourself and wear its badge. Badges usually belong to groups of people, not to single persons, although family badges were widely used in the Middle Ages, as will be explained in a moment.

7. *Greek soldier bearing round shield with device of snake*

Our modern Army, Navy and Air Force use badges to distinguish the different units and ships which make them up. Picture 8 shows the badge of a ship famous in naval history, H.M.S. *Ark Royal*. The charge is a Noah's ark, with a royal crown on top of it. A ship's rope forms the circle round the badge and the crown above is a naval crown, often used by ships and by families connected with the navy. It is made up of alternate square sails and sterns of ships.

8. *Badge of H.M.S.* Ark Royal

There have been four British ships bearing this name. The first, the Elizabethan *Ark Royal*, fought against the Spanish Armada in 1588. The second *Ark Royal* fought at the Dardanelles in the First World War, 1914–1918, and the third played an important part in the Second World War, until she was sunk by one of Hitler's submarines in 1941. The present *Ark Royal* is one of the biggest aircraft carriers in the Royal Navy.

The Air Forces of Britain and the Commonwealth countries also use a circular frame for their badges, with a crown above it. The name and number of the squadron is written round the badge and in the centre is the emblem belonging to the unit. The 1st Squadron of the Royal Indian Air Force has a tiger; the 6th Australian Squadron a boomerang.

9. *An Air Force badge*

10. *The badge of the Royal Corps of Signals*

11. *Yeoman warder of the Tower of London*

12. *The Prince of Wales's feathers*

Army badges are of great interest. Sometimes they contain charges connected with battles in which the regiment or unit has won honours, sometimes they carry old and historic emblems such as the Star of the Order of St. Patrick, which appears on the officers' caps of the Irish Guards, or the gold dragon of Wessex, used by the Wessex Division in the Second World War and said to have been borne on King Harold's banners at the Battle of Hastings.

The badge of the Royal Corps of Signals, shown here, is the figure of Mercury, the winged messenger.

In the Middle Ages, kings and noblemen possessed their own personal badges, which could be worn by their servants and carried on their property. The royal family still retains this custom today. The Yeoman Warders of the Tower of London, for instance, wear the Rose, Thistle and Shamrock of the United Kingdom.

One of the most familiar of royal badges is the one called "The Prince of Wales's feathers". It would be more correct to say that this is the badge used by the heir to the throne. Today this is, of course, H.R.H. Prince Charles, and he has been created Prince of Wales, but not all heirs to the throne have been given this title.

The ostrich feathers encircled by a coronet, as you see them in the picture below, were first used by Edward, the only son of King Henry the Eighth. He was, in fact, never created Prince of Wales, but he *was* heir to the throne and became King Edward the Sixth.

Before his time, the feathers were used as a badge in various ways, both by kings and royal princes. For instance, Edward the Black Prince, who fought against the French at Crécy in 1346, put the feathers on a black shield. He gained his nickname because of this, not because he wore black armour, as is sometimes said. His coat of arms is drawn and explained more fully on page 26.

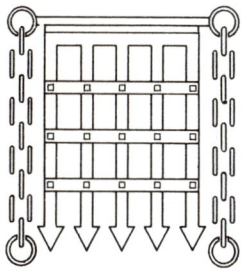

13. *The portcullis*

14. *The Tudor rose*

You often see the personal badges of kings and queens and noblemen carved on old buildings, pictured in stained glass, or displayed on their tombs in churches and cathedrals. Pictures 13 and 14 show two well-known Tudor badges, the portcullis and the rose. These were favourite badges of Henry the Seventh and Henry the Eighth, but they had been royal emblems for some time before the Tudors used them in the sixteenth century.

Henry the Seventh claimed the throne partly through his mother, Lady Margaret Beaufort. The Beauforts were descended from John of Gaunt, Duke of Lancaster, a son of Edward the Third, and one of the most powerful men of the fourteenth century. The portcullis was the badge of the Beauforts. The red rose belonged to the House of Lancaster, and was widely used by Lancastrians in the Wars of the Roses. Henry generally put a crown over both these family badges, to give them royal significance.

Another old royal badge is that of the white hart with a coronet round its neck. This was used by Richard the Second, the only son of the Black Prince. It is often found on inn signs, and you may have seen an example of it in your own part of the country. It was, and still is, common to use the arms and badges of noblemen and royal persons on inn signs. Two examples that are found all over England are "The Feathers" and "The Rose and Crown".

15. *The white hart*

The wild boar was the badge of Richard the Third, the king known as Crookback, who is said to have murdered the Princes in the Tower. He was killed at the Battle of Bosworth in 1485, and his crown taken by Henry Tudor. In his play, *Richard the Third*, Shakespeare uses the boar as a nickname for him. The Earl of Richmond, who leads the revolt against Richard, refers to the hated king as: "The wretched, bloody, and usurping boar" and "This foul swine"—words which mean a great deal more when you know that Richard's badge was a wild boar.

Noblemen also had their badges. If you live in the Midlands, you may well see one of the most famous, "the bear and ragged staff", which was the badge of the powerful Earls of Warwick, one of whom was known as "The Kingmaker". The badge appears today in the arms of the Warwickshire County Council. You can see these in colour on the opposite page. The three red crosses on this shield are of a special type, common in heraldry, and blazoned *cross crosslets*. They too are taken from the arms of the Earls of Warwick. The motto is borrowed from the arms of William Shakespeare, the county's most famous son. It is old French and means: Not without right. Shakespeare's shield carried a canting device: a spear. You can see it below.

16. *White swan ducally gorged*

Other badges have found their way into county arms. Picture 16 shows a white swan ducally gorged; this means that the swan has a duke's coronet around its neck. This was one of the badges of the Stafford family, Dukes of Buckingham, and you see their swan in the Buckinghamshire county arms, and in some town arms as well.

Picture 17 shows a rose within a sun's rays. This is called a *rose en soleil*. It was a favourite badge of the Yorkist king, Edward the Fourth, and now appears in the arms of the West Riding of Yorkshire.

17. *Rose en soleil*

I have told you something about badges first, because you are likely to see and possibly to recognise them more easily than shields. But badges are *not* coats of arms, and there is a very important difference between them and the charges on the shield. The difference is that the charges, in their particular colours, could be used *only* by members of the family, and were hereditary. This means that they were handed down from father to son. A badge, which is rarely used by families in modern times, could be worn by servants and men-at-arms of the estate. But although badges have a special place in heraldry, the most important thing is the coat of arms.

NON · SANS · DROICT

18. *The arms of Shakespeare*

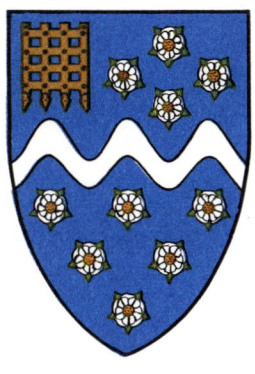

The Arms of Westminster Bank
(page 34)

The Arms of Warwickshire County Council
(page 12)

The Arms of the University of Sussex
(page 55)

4.

The Coat of Arms

19. *Knights from the Bayeux Tapestry*

We know that groups of men, such as tribes and army corps, have carried devices on shields and battle standards since long before the birth of Christ, but when did individuals begin to use their own emblems on tunic, shield, lance pennon and helmet?

This personal use of heraldry, in which every noble family had its own armorial bearings, grew up during the Middle Ages, roughly from the time of the Norman Conquest in 1066 to the reign of Henry the Seventh, which began in 1485. By the end of that four hundred years, heraldry was an important and established system used all over Europe, and governed by strict rules. In England the rules were enforced by the heralds who are described more fully in chapter 6.

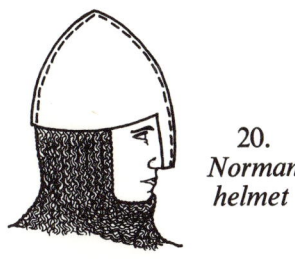

20. *Norman helmet*

A few of the Norman and English knights who fought at the Battle of Hastings carried devices on their shields and on the pennons of their lances, though it is not known whether these emblems belonged to the knight personally, or to a group of knights. You can see two heraldic shields in picture 19, which is copied from the Bayeux tapestry. The tapestry was a kind of strip picture woven in wool, made not long after the battle was fought.

21. *A great helm*

There was good reason for placing this kind of mark of identity on a shield or pennon. The helmet covered so much of the knight's face that his soldiers found it difficult to recognise their leader. The Norman helmet with its "nasal", or nosepiece, made it hard enough to see who a man was, and when, a little later, the great helm was invented, the knight's face was completely concealed. The two types of helmet are shown in pictures 20 and 21.

13

The armies of those days were very different from the forces of modern times. The men were not often in service for long, nor were they grouped into large units like regiments. Kings demanded from their noblemen so many horsemen and foot-soldiers, and the noblemen in their turn, demanded that the knights who held their manors should supply so many soldiers in time of war. This meant that men usually fought in small bands under their own leader, and it was therefore essential that they should recognise him easily. This was especially true of the large mixed armies which came from all over Europe to fight in the Crusades. Writers of the early Middle Ages usually refer to coats of arms as "cognizances", a word meaning "recognition" or mark of identity. This shows that armorial bearings had a practical purpose for the people of the time.

22. *Sir Roger de Trumpington's brass effigy, Trumpington, Cambridge. He died in 1289. Note the great helm beneath his head and his canting device of two trumpets*

The charges on the shields had to be simple and bold in design, so that they could be seen clearly. The earliest coats of arms often contain nothing more than a coloured bar, or a cross of some type, or a single animal such as a lion or a dragon. These charges were riveted on to the shield, which was made of metal, wood or boiled leather, called *cuir-bouilli*. This material was very hard and light, and was used not only for the shield but for parts of the armour, such as the "poleyns" which protected the knees. Sir Roger de Trumpington in picture 22 is wearing poleyns made of leather or of *cuir-bouilli*.

How did men acquire these coats of arms? In the early Middle Ages, kings and princes sometimes granted armorial bearings to their subjects for special reasons, but usually the wearer invented them for himself.

Fairly soon after the Norman Conquest, arms were adopted by individuals, and were treated as hereditary, that is, the owner considered them to be his personal property, to be passed on to his sons. This happened not only in Britain but all over Europe.

These early arms are sometimes called "arms of assumption" because the knight "assumed" or made them up for himself. The invention of arms, said a fourteenth century writer, "is lawful, just as names were invented to distinguish men." At first, only comparatively few families had their own arms, and it was not so likely that two men would choose the same devices. As more and more families "assumed" arms, however, difficulties arose. It was all too easy for two men, unknown to each other, to choose the same armorial bearings.

23. *The original Scrope and Grosvenor arms*

Many disputes must have taken place, and some are recorded in old documents. The most celebrated quarrel occurred in about 1385. King Richard the Second's army was mustering for a campaign against the Scots. One of the barons, Lord Scrope of Lancashire, saw that arms exactly like his own were being carried by Sir Robert Grosvenor, a mere knight from the neighbouring county of Cheshire.

Scrope was angry, for this was not the first time that he had met his arms on someone else's shield. A few years before, he had found a Cornishman named Carminow bearing them. Carminow had refused to give them up. He traced his ancestry back to the days of King Arthur, like many other good Cornishmen, and declared that Lord Scrope was only a newcomer in arms and descent, having come to England with the Normans in 1066. However, the matter was settled fairly peaceably by a small committee of knights, who decided that both Scrope and Carminow could keep the same arms. No doubt they hoped that the quarrel would be forgotten once Carminow had returned to his distant Cornish lands.

To see his arms displayed on the shield of Sir Robert Grosvenor was, however, too much for Lord Scrope. He took the matter to the High Court of Chivalry, which was a military court presided over by the Earl Marshal and the High Constable. The dispute lasted for five years, filled two volumes of records, and cost a fortune. Witnesses were gathered from all over England. They included such well-known Englishmen as John of Gaunt, Duke of Lancaster and the king's uncle, and Geoffrey Chaucer, the poet.

24. *Geoffrey Chaucer*

In the end, an appeal was made to the king himself. Lord Scrope won his case and kept his coat of arms, but he was almost ruined by the legal costs of the case.

15

25.
*The Grosvenor
arms*

Sir Robert Grosvenor adopted new armorial bearings, and these the Grosvenors carry to this day, when the head of the family is no longer a mere knight, but Duke of Westminster.

The wheatsheaf on the Grosvenor arms is blazoned in heraldry as a "garb". If you live in or near Cheshire, you will find that three garbs form the armorial bearings of the county, and the same device appears in the arms of Chester, for this is the county where the Grosvenors originally held their lands.

There have not been many disagreements of this kind since that expensive quarrel in 1385, but not very long ago, in 1954, a dispute arose between the Corporation of Manchester and a theatre, the Manchester Palace of Varieties. The Corporation's complaint was that the theatre had placed an embroidered copy of the City arms on the curtain pelmet above the stage, and that they used the arms as their Company seal. This was an important matter, for a seal is used on legal documents.

The Palace of Varieties refused to stop using the City arms in this way, so the Corporation asked the Earl Marshal to deal with the case. He acts for the Queen in matters of arms, and has the right to set up a Court of Chivalry, like the one that met to judge between Lord Scrope and Sir Robert Grosvenor. The Earl Marshal and his officers from the College of Arms were present, and the case was judged by the Lord Chief Justice of England.

The judge was not very concerned about the arms on the pelmet. After all, he said, hundreds of public houses display the arms of royal and noble persons, and nobody takes them to court for doing so. But he *was* concerned that the Palace of Varieties used the City arms as their seal. He therefore gave judgement against the theatre, forbidding them to use the arms in future, and ordering them to pay the costs of the case, which were three hundred pounds.

As this was the first time that the High Court of Chivalry had sat in England for over two hundred years, it was a great occasion for all who are interested in heraldry. Such disputes, however, have been very rare since the fifteenth century, for it was then that the practice of "assuming" arms was given up. The College of Arms was founded in 1484. Armorial bearings must be granted by its officers, and they make certain that the same arms are not carried by two different families, or by bodies such as theatres and companies.

16

5. Tournaments

26. *Jousting at a tournament*

It was not only in war that there was a danger that two men might be found carrying the same armorial bearings. Quarrels could easily have broken out on the tournament field if two of the competitors had borne the same devices on their shields or helmets.

During the Middle Ages, the tournament became an immensely important and popular institution. It consisted of a series of mock battles, performed partly for sport and partly as a serious training for war. Like any sport, it had its rules of fair play and honourable behaviour. The fights were called "jousts", and were fought by pairs of knights, each one trying to knock the other off his horse by a heavy blow from his lance.

Though this was done in sport, there was a serious side to jousting. Amid the endless warfare of the Middle Ages, men's savagery and cruelty was often enough displayed. The tournaments helped to strengthen the ideals of chivalry, which taught men to be truthful, courteous, generous to the weak, merciful to their enemies, and steadfast in battle. Though many may have failed to keep their vows of knighthood, there were undoubtedly some who tried to live up to the code of honour which is meant by the word "chivalry". These ideals play an important part in the poetry and tales written at the time, especially the stories of King Arthur and his knights of the Round Table.

27. *A jousting helmet*

28. *An heraldic banner*

Tournaments also had an important influence on heraldry. The very word "heraldry" belongs to the sport of jousting, for the heralds were, in the first place, men who organised tournaments. It was through their duties in summoning the combatants, proclaiming their names, and seeing that the rules were kept, that heralds became so expert about the armorial bearings of different families. It was at the tournament that knights really had a chance to display their heraldic devices in all their glory.

Apart from the armorial bearings on shields and tunics, the "trappers" or saddle-cloths of the horses were also embroidered with their owners' arms. The black horse's trapper in picture 29 is covered with scallop shells, the device of Lord Scales. Chargers were covered with these long flowing trappers, even in battle. They were not mere decoration. They were often padded, so that they acted as protection to the horse from thrusts of lance or sword.

In addition to the heraldic display on shield, surcoat and trapper, the jousting helmets of the combatants usually carried crests of painted wood or leather, and the tents that surrounded the field were often woven in their owners' colours and decorated with banners, like the one in picture 28.

If you live in London, you have probably heard of Smithfield, the great meat market. The name means "a smooth field" not a "field of smiths". Once it resounded with the clash of arms and the flourish of trumpets, for the meat lorries unload their beef and mutton on land where tournaments were held long ago.

On June 11th, 1467, a splendid royal tournament was held at Smithfield to celebrate the marriage of King Edward the Fourth to Elizabeth Wood-ville. The chief joust of the day was to be between the king's relative, Lord Scales, and a Frenchman, Count de la Roche.

Days had been spent in preparing the field. Down the centre was built a barrier of canvas and wood. The two knights were to ride at each other along each side of this fence. On three sides of the field stood covered or open wooden stands, in tiers, much as you see them today at a football ground. The tournament day was a public holiday and everyone in the city from apprentices to noblemen, crowded on to the field. They ate meat pies, drank beer or wine, gossiped and sang, while they were waiting for the tournament to begin. A flourish of trumpets announced the arrival of the king—"the handsomest man in Europe", as a Frenchman called him.

The heralds proclaimed the opening of the tournament and the names of the first contestants. Lord Scales and the French Count rode on to the field. Their horses began to canter towards each other, and with a clash of arms the two combatants met at the centre of the barrier.

The fight was over almost before it had begun. The Count's horse appeared to have been struck. It reared in the air, snorting and whinnying, and fell dead upon the field.

Confusion and shouting followed, for this was what would today be called a "foul". It was against the rules to strike your opponent's horse. While the angry Count de la Roche was helped to his feet, the Lord Constable made Lord Scales dismount and examined his armour and his horse. Underneath the saddle-cloth he found a metal spike, riveted on to the saddle. It was this that had struck the Count's horse, over the top of the barrier. Lord Scales was at once disqualified, and the King ordered a second day's holiday so that the two men could fight it out on foot. The combat next day, with axes and daggers, was so bitter that Edward rose from his seat and stopped the fight.

Thus ended a tournament that had given Londoners an extra day's holiday and filled the ale-houses with argument and gossip for some time to come.

29. *Lord Scales unseats the Count de la Roche*

30. *A herald in a tabard*

6. All Sorts of Heralds

"Hark the herald angels sing!" The Christmas hymn rolls out, and the "herald angels" bring each verse to an end with their message. These angelic heralds may not be bearing arms, but they are performing a duty that has always belonged to heralds: they are proclaiming news.

In the last chapter, we met the heralds on the tournament field, and in the early Middle Ages, their work was chiefly connected with the jousts. Kings and noblemen employed them to organise the sport for them.

First, an experienced herald, known as a King of Heralds, went into the district where the tournament was to be held, and proclaimed the day and place where it was to be, and the names of the chief combatants. When the jousting day arrived, the knights rode to the field, and the heralds announced their names to the waiting crowd. The great jousting helmets completely concealed the faces of the knights. It was the heralds who recognised them by their arms, and proclaimed who they were. Many noblemen employed their own heralds, and these answered questions about their masters, boasted of their bravery, and cheered them on as they fought.

Also connected with the tournaments were the king's chief military officers, his High Constable and Earl Marshal. These two men presided over tournaments, and had to have a wide knowledge of armorial bearings. They had their own military court, the High Court of Chivalry, where they settled disputes. This was where the quarrel between Lord Scrope and Sir Robert Grosvenor was heard, and, hundreds of years later, the dispute between the Manchester Corporation and the Palace of Varieties.

There is no longer a High Constable of England, though we still use the word "constable" for a policeman. There is, however, an Earl Marshal. This office is always held by the Duke of Norfolk, who is the "Premier Duke", or most senior nobleman in England.

When an army was mustered for battle, a list was made of those present, and sometimes each man's coat of arms was recorded as well. Lists of those taking part in tournaments were also kept in the same way. In many cases the shields and banners were illustrated in colour.

These early records are called "rolls of arms", because they were written on long strips of parchment, and rolled up. Many of them must have been compiled by those experts in armorial bearings, the heralds. These documents go back to the thirteenth century, and in some cases were copied more than once, so that several versions of them exist. The British Museum and the College of Arms possess a number of them.

A particularly interesting roll of arms is "The Siege of Caerlaverock". It is written in verse and was composed about 1300 to celebrate an actual battle.

In July, 1300, King Edward the First led an expedition against Scotland. He besieged the Castle of Caerlaverock, near Dumfries. The poem contains descriptions of the arms of those who took part. Here is one of them. The words are translated from French.

"Prince and Duke and all men else held John FitzMarmaduke in praise;
He on banner red a fess bore, white between three popinjays."

You have met the band called a fess on page 8.

31. *The arms of Montbouchier*

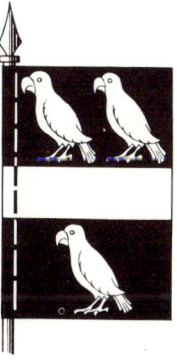

32. *The arms of FitzMarmaduke*

The battle is described in detail:

"Timely came the ships with stores and engines; then the foot-men bold
Forward went discharging arrows, bolts and stones against the hold.
Then were seen such hurtling stones as caps and helms would pound to dust,
Shatter shields and batter targes [round shields]; kill and wound was now
     their lust;
And great shouts arose whenever any damage was revealed.
First came Bertram de Montbouchier, who on shining silver shield
Bore three pitchers, red in colour, in a bordure black, with bezants;
With him, Gerard de Gondronville, active knight of handsome presence."

You can guess that "bordure" means a border, and that the bezants are the small round objects. They are more fully described on page 37.

The defenders of Caerlaverock fought bravely, but their losses were heavy. When they surrendered to the king, only sixty of them were left. The poem says that the king, true to the ideals of chivalry, had mercy on them. He even gave each one of them new clothes.

As time went on, heralds took over more duties than simply organising tournaments, and keeping records of those present at a joust or a battle. They became such trusted and experienced servants of kings and noblemen that they were often used to carry messages and letters. In times of war, they became ambassadors between the opposing sides.

As the heralds were recognised as the greatest experts in armorial bearings, they were at last formed into an official body, the College of Arms. This was in 1484. Soon after this, they began to hold regular investigations all over England. The senior heralds, the Kings of Arms, divided England into different regions, and each inspected a region, to see that every man who used a coat of arms really had a right to it. These inspections were called "Visitations", and it is from them, as well as from the Rolls of Arms, that we learn much about heraldry and its rules.

The Earl Marshal presides over the College of Arms, which has thirteen permanent officers. First come the three Kings of Arms. Garter King of Arms is responsible for the Order of the Garter, a high honour founded by Edward the Third, and given to men who have performed outstanding services to the country. The other two Kings of Arms divide England between them. Norroy King of Arms has authority over the north of England and Northern Ireland; Clarenceux King of Arms deals with the southern and western counties. Wales is the responsibility of Garter King of Arms.

33. *The shield of the College of Arms. The birds are doves "with dexter wings elevated"*

Then come the six heralds. They still bear the names given them centuries ago, names taken for the most part from royal castles: Windsor, Richmond, Somerset, York, Lancaster and Chester. These heralds are addressed as "The Richmond Herald", "The York Herald", and so on.

A man training to be a herald is called a "pursuivant" because he is "pursuing" his way to being a full herald. The four pursuivants take their names from old badges: Rouge Dragon, Rouge Croix, Bluemantle and Portcullis.

The Earl Marshal, assisted by the officers of the College of Arms, is responsible for the organisation of import-

22

34. *A medieval herald's tabard*

ant state ceremonies, such as a coronation or a state funeral. On these occasions, the heralds are in attendance upon the sovereign. They wear their tabards, which are loose-fitting tunics, embroidered back and front and on the shoulder-pieces, with the royal arms.

Scottish heraldry is governed by different officers. The chief position is held by the Lord Lyon King of Arms. He is a judge, which is why he is called "Lord Lyon", and only the Queen addresses him without this title. She calls him Our Lyon King of Arms.

The Scottish Court of Chivalry over which he presides is known as the Lyon Court, and is held in Edinburgh. The three Scottish heralds are called Marchmont, Rothsaye and Albany, and the three pursuivants, Dingwall, Unicorn and Carrick.

The College of Arms stands in Queen Victoria Street, in the city of London. If you think that your family has the right to bear arms, the officials of the College will look into their records and tell you. Much of the herald's work today takes the form of tracing the pedigrees of families. If you cannot prove that your family has a coat of arms, you can apply for a new grant of arms. It will cost you over a hundred pounds. You will receive a beautifully lettered document called a Patent. This will have your armorial bearings painted upon it, and will entitle you and your descendants to carry arms.

Not many private persons do this today, unless they are created knights or peers, but new universities, societies and corporations of all kinds apply for grants of arms. The College officials design these for them, and generally choose charges which have some connection with the society or corporation which requires the arms.

35. *The shield of the National Coal Board*

This is the shield of the National Coal Board. The diamond-shaped charges across the middle have been used in coats of arms for hundreds of years and are called *fusils*. Here, they were chosen to represent coal.

23

7. The Achievement

36. *A gentleman's helmet*

The whole coat of arms, with shield, helmet and crest, is called the *achievement*. This is what is usually displayed on church tombs and monuments, or over the porch of an old house, or on an inn sign.

The shield is the most important item. It carries the colours and charges which belong to the family, the "marks of identity" by which you recognised a man.

Above the shield and resting on top of it, is sometimes a *helmet of rank*. There are several different types and positions for the helmet, which show the rank of nobility to which the owner belongs. Sometimes he is not a nobleman at all, but an esquire, or gentleman. The helmet that you are most likely to see is the gentleman's type shown in picture 36 and this is also used by societies and bodies like town councils. In some cases the vizor, a hinged plate covering the upper part of the face, is shown, and, for a gentleman's helmet, this must be shut. A knight or baronet uses the same type of helmet, but in their case, it is placed "affronté", facing you, and the vizor is open. As the inside of the helmet is painted red, this gives rather an ugly impression of a gaping mouth, as in picture 37.

37. *A knight's helmet*

The use of helmets of rank belongs to the later history of heraldry. You will find many achievements that do not follow these rules, or that have no helmet at all.

38. *A crest resting on a wreath of the colours*

The *crest* is placed above the helmet, or directly above the shield. It is usually shown resting on a twisted scarf, called a *wreath of the colours*, or a *torse*. It can also rest on a cap called a *chapeau*, which is described at the end of this chapter. The colours of the torse are usually the two chief colours appearing on the shield. Picture 38 shows a crest, resting on a torse, or wreath of the colours.

When a knight really wore a crest, as he did in a tournament, it was bolted on to the top of his helmet.

It needed to be as light as possible, so it was made of wood, or *cuir-bouilli* (boiled leather), or of stuffed leather. You can see a helmet with a crest in picture 40 below. Sometimes you will see a helmet, with its crest, hanging on the wall above a tomb in a church, and there may be other parts of armour too, such as steel gauntlets. These are unlikely to be older than about 1600. But on stone tombs, helmets and crests are often carved, and the figure of the knight may also be wearing a surcoat with his arms carved upon it, and be carrying an heraldic shield on his left arm.

It is worth looking carefully at tombs. At first glance, they may seem broken, dusty, even rather boring, but if you look at them more closely, you may find that they have interesting details of armour and heraldry. You can very quickly learn the three main types of armour, and these are a guide to the period when the knight lived.

39. *Sir John d'Aubernon died* 1327 (*Stoke D'Abernon Church, Surrey*)

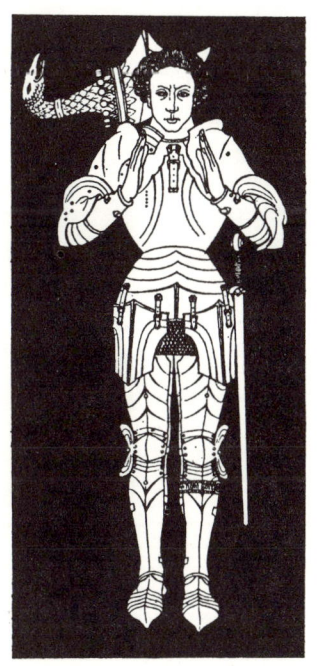

40. *Richard Beauchamp, Earl of Warwick, died* 1439 (*St. Mary's Church, Warwick*)

For instance, the oldest and probably the most battered figures will be wearing *chain-mail*, with a hood of mail fitting over their heads, close round their faces. This shows that they lived in the twelfth or early thirteenth century, the time of King John, Richard Cœur de Lion and Thomas à Becket.

If they have some *plate* armour on their arms and legs, like Sir John d'Aubernon in picture 39, they belong to the period roughly between 1250 and 1400, the centuries when England fought the Welsh and the Scots, under Edward the First, Second and Third; the time when the Hundred Years War against France began, and the battles of Crécy and Poitiers were fought.

During this period, more and more plate was being added to armour, and from about 1420 onwards, when the Wars of the Roses took place, the knight was almost entirely encased in steel plate armour as in picture 40. Knights of all these periods can be seen on tombs. In many cases the great helm will be lying underneath their heads, acting as a pillow.

25

41. *The Black Prince*

42. *The Black Prince's arms for peace*

Not many real helmets, crests or embroidered surcoats have survived from the Middle Ages. However, if you visit Canterbury Cathedral you can see some of the oldest in England. Edward the Black Prince was buried in the Cathedral in 1376, and his equipment was hung over his tomb: his helmet and crest, his shield, gauntlets and sword, and his surcoat embroidered with the royal arms. The colours have now faded almost to nothing, but in 1954 a complete set of equipment was made and put in the cathedral, so that you can see what it really would have looked like when the Prince wore it, about six hundred years ago.

His shield and surcoat show the royal arms of that time, with lions and fleurs-de-lys, but on the side of his tomb there appears a different shield, known as his "shield for peace". This is black, with the three white ostrich feathers which later became the official badge for the heir to the throne. You may remember from Chapter 3 that it was this black shield that most likely gave him his nickname of "the Black Prince".

Going back to the achievement which you may see above a tomb, or painted on an inn sign, the helmet usually has a pair of cloth streamers attached to it, spreading out on either side of the shield. These are called the *mantling*, and may have once served a practical purpose, protecting the knight's neck from the direct rays of the sun. A helmet was extremely hot and heavy to wear, especially over a chain-mail hood, and crusading knights may well have adopted the idea from the Saracens against whom they fought under the hot sun of the Holy Land.

In heraldry, the mantling is often very decorative. It flows out on each side of the shield, and, like the wreath, is usually painted in the two chief colours used in the coat of arms.

In picture 45 on the opposite page, you can see the mantling on the royal arms flowing out from under the crown on either side of the helmet.

43. *A Saracen*

26

If you visit Windsor Castle and St. George's Chapel, you will see some of the finest examples of achievements in England. They are coloured plaques, placed on the panelling behind the choir stalls of the chapel, and show the arms of many of the Knights of the Most Noble Order of the Garter.

The Order of the Garter was founded by King Edward the Third in 1348. It consists of twenty-five Knights Companions, the Sovereign and members of the royal family, and some foreign monarchs. The late Sir Winston Churchill was created a Knight of the Garter, the highest honour that can be granted in the United Kingdom. At his state funeral, the insignia of the Order were laid upon his coffin. They are the Garter itself, a band of blue velvet, inscribed with the motto: *Honi soit qui mal y pense* (Evil be to him who thinks evil of it); the gold and enamel Collar, with the figure of St. George slaying the dragon hanging from it; the silver Star, with the red St. George's cross in the centre.

The garter

The collar

The star

44. *Garter insignia*

45. *The Royal Arms*

Picture 45 shows the royal arms. You will see that they are encircled by the Garter, for the sovereign is always a member of the Order.

The quarters of the shield show the three lions passant of England, the lion rampant of Scotland, and the harp of Ireland. Above the helmet and crown stands the lion which has been the royal crest for seven centuries. Notice the *ermine* on the mantling. You will meet this fur again in the next chapter.

The lion and unicorn which hold up the shield are its *supporters*.

Supporters are only granted to royal persons and noblemen, and to some bodies such as councils and companies. The figures may be animals or humans, or mythical creatures such as dragons or sea-horses. The Corporation of Penzance in Cornwall, for instance, has a fisherman on one side, and a pirate on the other; Sheffield City arms has Thor and Vulcan, gods of thunder and armour; the late Lord Beaverbrook had two beavers; Lord Brabazon, well-known in the motoring and flying world, has two sea-gulls, holding the shield in their beaks and rising with it above the water. See how many pictures of achievements with supporters you can find in this book.

If a family possesses a motto, it is written on a scroll and placed beneath the shield. In England and Wales, you may choose what motto you please, and it does not form part of your achievement, officially. It can be changed without reference to the College of Arms. Here are three well-known mottoes:

The B.B.C.: "Nation shall speak peace unto nation."
The Prince of Wales: "Ich Dien" (I serve).
The Royal Arms: "Dieu et mon droit" (God and my right).

In Scotland, the motto *is* part of the achievement, and is used far more. It often appears on a banner, carried in the paws either of the animal of the crest, or of one of the supporters. It may contain the name of the chief of the clan or a branch of it, like "A Hume, a Hume". Sometimes the words are taken from an old secret password used by the clansmen, like "I am reddie."

46. *The Drummond badge*

As was said in the chapter about badges, members of a Scottish clan may use the chief's crest as a badge, surrounded by a strap bearing the chief's motto. Picture 46 shows the Drummond badge. The motto, "Gang warily", meaning "Go carefully", has an interesting history. At the Battle of Bannockburn in 1314, the Scots scattered metal spikes called "caltraps" on the ground, to lame the horses of the English knights. This cruel but cunning idea was proposed by the Chief of Clan Drummond, whose successors became the Earls of Perth. Their motto, "Gang warily", has some purpose to it, therefore.

The Drummond shield is strewn with caltraps, and the arms of Stirlingshire, where the Battle of Bannockburn took place, have a caltrap at the top and bottom (see picture 48). These arms also have the diagonal cross of St. Andrew called a "saltire", which is common in Scottish heraldry, as St. Andrew is Scotland's patron saint.

A crest is sometimes set on a *chapeau* instead of a wreath of the colours. The *chapeau* is a soft cap, usually red turned back with ermine. It is a sign of authority, and it still has this old meaning when it is carried upon a cushion in front of the Queen on state occasions such as the opening of Parliament.

47. *A chapeau*

48. *The arms of Stirlingshire. The star-like charges on either side are pierced mullets. See glossary*

Crowns and coronets appear on achievements, but they are rather confusing, for they are used in several different ways. They may simply be used as one of the charges on the shield. When, however, one of them appears immediately above the shield, it shows the title of the owner, for there is a different type for every rank, from king and prince, to duke, earl and baron. Royal crowns have changed during the centuries, and you may well see different types if you look at old royal coats of arms in churches or on buildings. All, however, are distinguished from the coronets of noblemen by having bars arched over the top.

In addition to crowns and coronets of rank, there are several other types of crown, of which the two commonest are the mural crown, which is like an embattled wall, and is often used in town arms, and the naval crown, which frequently appears in the arms of sailors, and on ships' badges. There is one on page 9 (*Ark Royal*).

Modern royal

Earl

Mural

Duke

49. *Crowns and coronets*

8. What's on the Shield?

The arms in picture 50 are blazoned: Sable, three mullets argent, two and one. As you see, the field or background is black, the charges white. This illustrates an important colour rule of heraldry, explained in this chapter.

50. *"Sable, three mullets argent, two and one"*

As you read in chapter four, men "assumed" or invented their arms at first, but this was not quite such a free-for-all as it sounds. Heraldry very quickly developed rules which were generally accepted by knights all over Europe. Roads were bad and travel slow and difficult, but men were not so cut off from each other as is sometimes supposed. Two things in particular gave them frequent opportunities of meeting not only their fellow-countrymen, but knights from other countries. These were the tournaments and the wars, especially the Crusades. When men meet together, new ideas are exchanged and spread rapidly. The system of heraldry soon became common to the whole of Europe, with only minor national variations.

An important part of the system was the set of rules that govern the colours of the field and the charges.

Colours are divided into two groups:

1. The METALS	*or*	=	gold
	argent	=	silver (or white)
2. The TINCTURES	*gules*	=	red
	vert	=	green
	sable	=	black
	azure	=	blue
	purpure	=	purple

As well as the metals and tinctures, a FUR can be used. If this sounds strange, you have to remember that fur was very commonly used on clothing in the Middle Ages, and the fur on a shield is not intended to be real, but is a formal heraldic design, suggesting the coat of the animal. The two furs used are *ermine* and *vair*.

The ermine is another name for the Arctic stoat. In summer it has a coat of reddish brown, but in winter it moults and grows a white coat with a black-tipped tail. This fur was greatly valued and used by persons of rank.

In heraldry ermine is shown as a white field, covered with rows of black *ermine spots,* as they are called, which represent the black tips of the tails. These "spots" are drawn in several different ways. Three ways are shown in picture 51.

Sometimes the colours are reversed—white ermine spots on a black field. This is called *ermines.*

51. *Three types of ermine spots*

Vair was a fur used by those who could not afford ermine. It was squirrel fur. The original English squirrel was not the red one, but a blue-grey animal, with a white under-belly. If you imagine a number of the skins sewn together to make a cloak, you can see that they would be a kind of checkerboard of grey and white. The heraldic artists invented a formal pattern of blue and white shapes called *vair-bells.* You would hardly guess that they had squirrel skins in mind, it is so geometrical. The shields in pictures 52 and 53 belong to two ancient and well-known noble families, and show the use of the two furs.

The Sackville shield is blazoned: quarterly or and gules, a bend vair. This means: a field divided into quarters of gold and red, with a diagonal bar of vair.

The creatures which support the arms on either side of this shield are leopards. The Latin motto means: "Never undertake to do what you cannot carry out". You probably notice that the shield is a different shape from others in this book. Artists and carvers pleased themselves, and, after about 1600, when shields were no longer used in battle, they appear in many different and often highly decorative forms.

The Sackville family have played a long and important part in English history. They are said to have come over with William the Conqueror, and eventually rose in rank to be the Dukes of Dorset.

52. *The arms of the Sackvilles, Earls of Dorset*

The Sackvilles were particularly powerful during the reign of Queen Elizabeth. Sir Thomas Sackville was one of the men chosen to break the news to Mary Queen of Scots that Elizabeth had signed her death warrant, and that she was to be beheaded. Later, at the time of the Armada, this Sir Thomas was Lord Lieutenant of Sussex, and responsible for guarding much of the south coast against invasion by the Spaniards. At the end of his life, he put a tax on tobacco, because he believed, as many doctors do today, that it was bad "for the Healthe of a great nomber of our People."

The arms of Bowes are blazoned: ermine, three bows bent and stringed, palewise in fess, gules. This means: on an ermine field, three bows bent and stringed, upright across the centre, coloured red.

The Bowes family belong to the north of England. One branch of it married into the Lyon family, and these were the ancestors of the present Queen Mother, whose maiden name was Lady Elizabeth Bowes-Lyon.

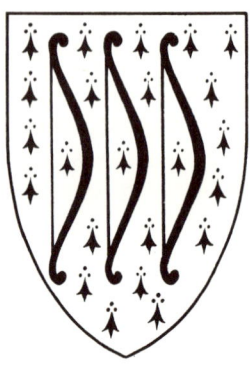

53. *The arms of Bowes*

The shield can be divided into two colours, and it is then called *parted* or *party*. Picture 54 shows the *party lines* which divide the shield, each with its special name.

Party per fess

per pale

Now we come to the colour rule mentioned at the beginning of the chapter. A metal must not be placed next to or upon a metal, or a tincture on a tincture. Therefore, if you divide the shield, the colours on each half must be one metal and one tincture. The same rule applies

per bend

per chevron

per saltire

per cross

54. *Party lines*

to the charges placed upon the field. A fur can be placed with either, however. You may occasionally come across a shield that does not keep to these rules. This almost certainly means that the arms are very old ones, devised before the rules were generally known and accepted.

Different areas of the shield have their special heraldic names. The right hand side is the *dexter* and the left the *sinister*, but they are the other way round from what you would expect. You have to think what would be right and left if you were actually carrying the shield on your arm, not looking at it from the front. (See picture 55).

Everything that is put on a shield is a *charge*. Some of these, which are among the oldest, are very simple, and are so common that they form a group on their own, called the *ordinaries*.

The heraldic names for them are easy to understand, for all except the first are related to the words used for party lines, shown in picture 54. The exception is the *chief*, which is called this because it is placed in the "chief" or upper part of the shield, which is the place of honour.

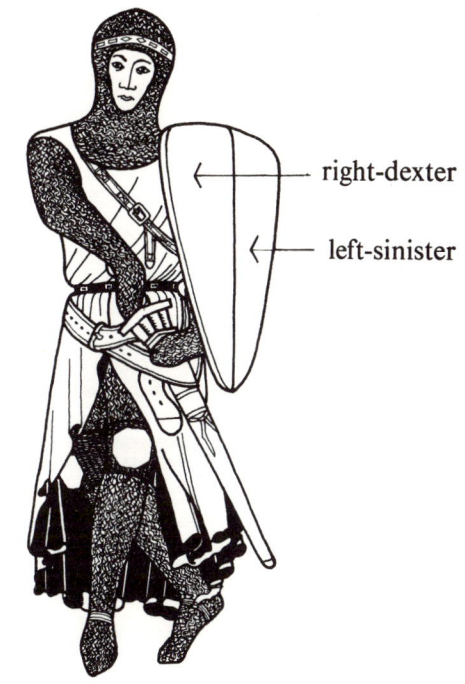

right-dexter

left-sinister

55. *Dexter and sinister*

Chief

Fess

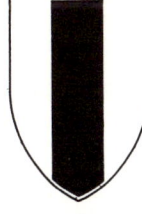

Pale

Bend

Chevron

Saltire

56. *The ordinaries*

Most of the party lines and ordinaries can be varied in a number of ways, which add to the beauty of the shield. Picture 57 shows the most common variations of line.

A fine example of a shield with a *fess wavy*, and one which you will probably be able to see in your own town, is that of the Westminster Bank. It is shown in colour opposite page 12. The blue field is *semé* or "strewn" with roses, and has a portcullis on it. Both these charges were, you may remember, favourite badges of the Tudor monarchs. The Bank has taken them from the arms of the City of Westminster, where they are reminders of Henry the Seventh, who added to Westminster Abbey the magnificent chapel which bears his name.

The blazon of the Bank's shield is: Azure, semé of roses argent, barbed and seeded proper, a fess wavy also argent, in the quarter a portcullis or. ("Proper" means "in its natural colour").

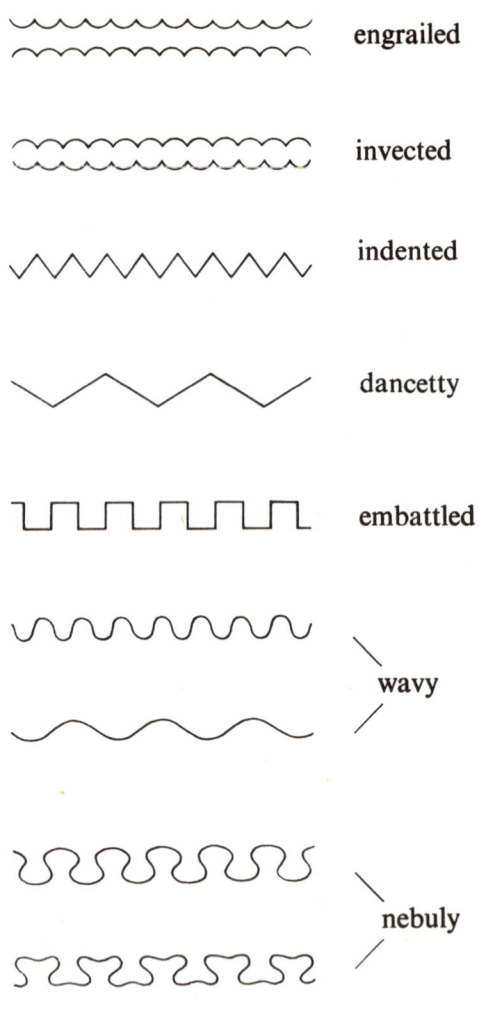

engrailed

invected

indented

dancetty

embattled

wavy

nebuly

57. Variations of lines

58. The arms of Fox-Davies

The shield on the left shows a *fess dancetty*. As only half the sun's face appears, it must be called a "demi-sun", and as it is sending forth rays, it must be blazoned, in full, as a "demi-sun in his splendour". To this must be added the words: "issuant from base", to show the position of the demi-sun on the shield.

Here are some other pictures in the book which illustrate ordinaries with varied lines:

A fess wavy—picture 95 (page 51)
A cross engrailed—picture 82 (page 47)
A chevron embattled—picture 91 (page 50)

The cross was not included with the other ordinaries in picture 56 because it is so important that it deserves a section of its own. It is, of course, a religious emblem. As an heraldic charge, it increased in use and variety during the Crusades. Pope Urban the Second, at the time of the First Crusade in 1095, decreed that the crusading soldiers should wear a red cross on their breasts and shoulders, as a token that they served Christ.

There are many different types of crosses used in arms. Five of them are shown below.

The word *moline* may have some connection with a mill. The round mill-stone had a piece of iron clamped at its centre, in shape very like this cross. The cross *flory* is so called because each limb ends in fleur-de-lys, a charge which you can see on the next page. The word *paté* is related to "paws". The cross has widely splayed ends, like the paws of an animal.

You may have seen the *Maltese cross* on ambulances belonging to the St. John's Ambulance Brigade. Their society is an old one. It goes back to the Knights of St. John of Jerusalem, an Order founded soon after the First Crusade in 1099. Its members were pledged to protect pilgrims, and care for the sick and wounded. They came to be known as Hospitallers. Later, the knights had their headquarters on the island of Malta, from which their white, eight-pointed cross takes its name.

Moline

Flory

Paté or formy

Maltese

Crosslet

59. *Crosses*

60. *Canton*

61. *Bordure*

Two other fairly common ordinaries are the *canton*, and the *bordure*. The canton is a small square in the top left hand corner of the shield, or to put it correctly, the *dexter corner in chief*. The bordure is a band round the edge of the shield. Both these small ordinaries often carry other charges, like the fleurs-de-lys, billets, or roundels that are shown in picture 62, and known as *sub-ordinaries*.

Of these, the fleur-de-lys is one of the best-known charges in heraldry. The medieval arms of France were an azure field, covered with gold fleurs-de-lys. King Edward the Third claimed that he was the rightful king of France, and, to make his claim plain to all, he divided his shield into four quarters, and put the French fleurs-de-lys in two of the quarters. (See page 58). Innumerable Englishmen used the device on their shields, and it appears in many county and city arms. The arms of Erith, in picture 97, have both a fleur-de-lys and a canton.

The other sub-ordinaries are taken, for the most part, from objects that were in common use in medieval times. The *mullet* or *molet* looks like a star, but it is really the pricking part of a spur. *Billet* is an old word for a piece of wood, which the charge resembles. The shape of the *fusil* was probably suggested by the spindle, something that would have been found in every medieval home. You have already met it on the arms of the National Coal Board on page 23.

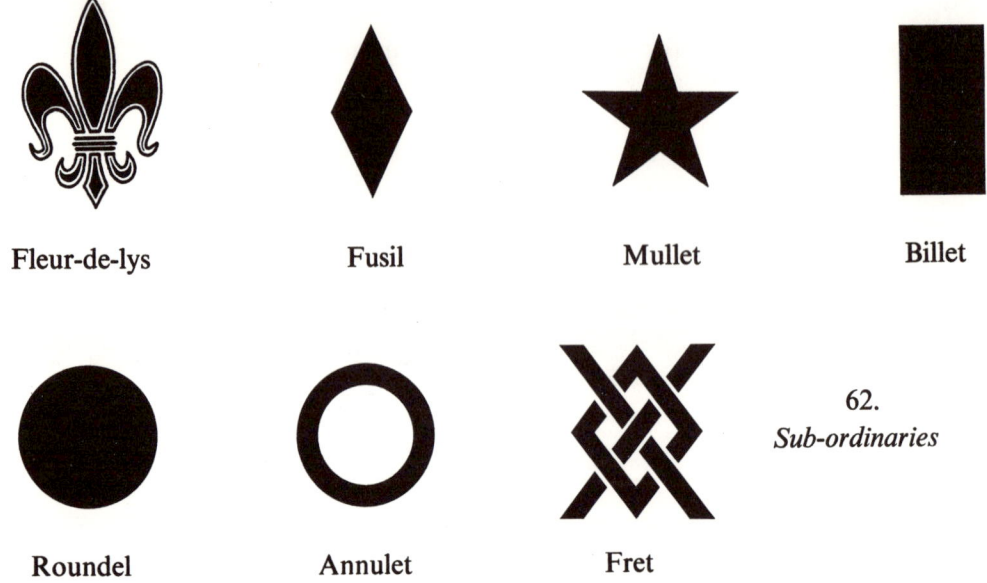

Fleur-de-lys   Fusil   Mullet   Billet

Roundel   Annulet   Fret

62. *Sub-ordinaries*

All these ordinaries and sub-ordinaries can be used in any of the metals or tinctures, but the *roundels* have special names for each colour, and rather interesting ones:

A roundel *or* is called a *bezant*	The Crusaders brought back from Byzantium gold coins. The word "bezant" may be taken from the name of the city.
A roundel *argent* is called a *plate*	This is also probably the name of a coin. The silver pieces of Spain were called "plates".
A roundel *azure* is called a *hurt*	This word comes from "hurtleberry" or "whortle-berry", a blue-black fruit.
A roundel *gules* is called a *tort*	A round cake or tart.
A roundel *sable* is called a *pellet* or *gunstone*	In other words, a cannon-ball.
A roundel *vert* is a *pomme*	*Pomme* is French for "apple".

There is one more roundel, this time with wavy blue and white bars across it. It is called a *fountain*.

A few of the ordinaries and sub-ordinaries can be used to cover the whole shield, and form a field on which other charges may be placed. For instance:

A field paly is covered with vertical bars or *pales*.
A field barry is covered with horizontal bars, each a little narrower than a fess.
A field bendy is covered with diagonal bars, or *bends*.
A field chevrony is entirely covered with *chevrons*.
A field fusily is entirely covered with *fusils*.

When a field is made up of small squares, like a draughts-board, it is called *checky*. If it is criss-crossed with narrow, interlacing bars, it is called *fretty*. Picture 63 shows the trellis-work effect of a fretty field. Robert Willoughby fought in the battle of Caerlaverock, and carried a shield fretty, blue and gold. The poem records that in his eagerness he threw his shield away, and received an arrow in his breast.

63. *Willoughby's shield*

A field or a charge may be covered with rows of small objects, and is then said to be *semé* or "powdered" with them. It can be "semé of roses" or "semé of scallopshells". If billets or crosses are used, the field is simply called "billetty" or "crusily", without the word "semé". If covered with fleurs-de-lys, then the field is "semé-de-lys".

Roundels covering a field or charge make it bezanty, platy, pommy, hurty, torty or pelletty. There is a field platy in picture 96.

Another very small device used to cover shields or charges is an object drawn like a rain-drop. Anything sprinkled with these is called *goutté*. The arms of the town of Wallsend in picture 64 are *goutté d'or*, covered with gold drops. Every charge on this shield has a meaning. Wallsend stands at the eastern end of Hadrian's wall, near the border between Scotland and England. The wall at the base of the shield is a reminder of this, and the eagle stands for the Romans who built the wall, for the eagle was used as the insignia of the legions. The black field and gold drops represent the local coal and copper-smelting industries.

64. The arms of Wallsend

The blazon of this shield is: Sable, goutté d'or, in base an embattled wall; thereon an eagle with wings displayed, both or.

9. The Charges

As more and more families used coats of arms, new ways of varying the shield had to be found. One very common method was to put one device upon another. The imaginary arms in picture 65 show a bend with a sword placed upon it. There are several other pictures in this book where an ordinary, like a bend or a chief or a fess, is charged with some device.

To ring the changes, more and more charges were introduced, some of them most unusual ones. Animals

65. On a bend, a sword point upwards

were favourite devices, from noble lions down to such humble creatures as hedgehogs. Birds, fish and insects of many kinds found their way on to coats of arms, until a kind of heraldic zoo was created.

Flowers, leaves, trees and fruits are many and varied. They are often used in canting arms: acorns for the Oakleys, as you saw in chapter two, apples for the Appletons, pears for the Perrys.

Then comes a large group which some heraldists call the *common charges*, objects which belonged to the daily life of the Middle Ages. Among them are devices as varied as castles, guns, arrows, anchors, windmills, stirrups, cups, hunting-horns and the tools of many trades. Most of them are easily recognisable. The more unusual ones have been given a chapter to themselves.

As animals were early favourites upon the shield, we will look first at the king of beasts, the lion.

The heraldic artists were not interested in making an exact zoological likeness of him. In fact, it is very unlikely that they had ever seen one in the earlier days of heraldry. The lion appears very often in an upright position, front paws raised, a position he could hardly use in real life, but which was particularly well fitted to the long narrow shield of the early Middle Ages. This position is called *rampant*. He is also found lying, standing, sitting and walking, and all these positions have their special names. Notice the word "guardant" must be added if he turns his head to face you. If he is looking over his shoulder behind him, he is termed "reguardant".

statant

sejant

couchant

66. *Heraldic lions*

sejant affronté

rampant guardant

passant

39

Lions appear in different colours, and their teeth, claws and tongues are often given a colour different from their bodies. The gold lions on the royal coat of arms have blue teeth, claws and tongues, which is blazoned: armed and langued azure.

Other wild animals often used in heraldry are bears, elephants, leopards, boars and wolves.

67. *A talbot passant*

Hunting was one of the chief sports of the Middle Ages, so dogs are frequently used on shields. Spaniels, terriers, blood-hounds and bulldogs all appear, but the oldest and most popular breeds were the foxhound and greyhound. They are recognisable by their ears. The foxhound has wide, drooping ears; the greyhound short, pricked ones. The foxhound was known as the *talbot*, and this name often appears on inn signs. Next time you see a Talbot Hotel, look and see if the sign shows a foxhound. It probably will.

The stag or hart is shown with branching antlers, called in heraldry *attires*. Stags' heads, and even antlers alone, are frequently found as charges. When a deer is shown without antlers, it represents the female, or hind.

68. *The crest of Ireland*

When deer or other animals are drawn with a collar and chain, or a coronet, round their necks, they are said to be *gorged*. We now use this word to mean "stuffed with food", but "gorge" is really the French word for "throat". Richard the Second's white hart badge in picture 15 is "gorged and chained".

The different positions of deer have special names, and very accurate and picturesque ones. The word *courant* is generally used for a running animal, but deer are given the term *at speed*. When a stag lies down, he is *lodged*: when he walks he is *trippant*. When he stands, he is *statant*, like the lion, but when he turns his head to face you, he is *at gaze*. When he leaps up on his hind legs, he is *springing*. The crest of Ireland (picture 68) shows a hart springing from the portal of a castle.

Horses and other domestic animals, such as cattle and goats, appear as charges, and one farmyard creature, the sheep, is so widely used in arms that he deserves a special mention to himself. As well as appearing in a standing position, very much as he does in a field, the sheep has two other important uses in heraldry.

69. *A fleece*

This is *not* a sheep suspended on a metal ring. It represents the sheepskin only, or *fleece*. For centuries, wool was one of the mainstays of England's wealth, and it is not surprising that the fleece appears in a large number of coats of arms, especially those of towns and counties which depended on wool for much of their trade. A fleece is usually coloured *or* (gold) to signify wealth.

The lamb is quite as common. It has a symbolic meaning for Christians, for Christ is often referred to as the "Lamb of God". The Holy Lamb can be found in many church carvings, as well as in heraldry. It is also called the *Pascal lamb*, Pasque being the French for Easter, and the *Agnus Dei*, which is Latin for "Lamb of God".

70. *The Pascal lamb*

It is always drawn passant (walking), with a flag of St. George on a cross staff over its right shoulder. A halo is drawn round its head. Like so many other heraldic charges, it is used on inn signs. You may have seen inns called "The Lamb and Flag".

The king of birds is the eagle, and, since the time of the Roman Empire, it has been a royal symbol in European heraldry. For hundreds of years much of Europe was known as the Holy Roman Empire, and the emperors used eagles as their insignia. If you travel to the Continent, you are certain to see examples of this royal bird, for it is used in the arms of many towns and provinces. Picture 71 on the next page shows the coat of arms of Merano, a city in Northern Italy, which was once a part of the Austrian Empire. The eagle was the emblem of the Austrian royal family.

71. *The arms of Merano*

72. *A martlet*

73. *A pelican
in her piety*

In this shield, the eagle is *gules* (red). With wings outspread, and head turned to its right, the eagle is termed *displayed*.

A small bird very frequently used in arms is the swallow, known heraldically as the *martlet*. It is generally drawn without proper feet, as in picture 72. The skimming flight of swallows gave rise to the popular belief that they never perched anywhere, because they had no feet to perch on.

Other birds make frequent appearances on the shield and crest: hawks, doves, ravens, swans, blackbirds and choughs. Some of these appear later on in the book and are more fully described with the coats of arms in which they are used.

Two other birds with curious legends attached to them are the pelican and the crane. The pelican is not only used in heraldry, but was a favourite subject of the church carvers. You will see it on pulpits, choir-stalls and bench-ends in many old churches, but you may not recognise it for a pelican. It is never shown with the big pouch hanging from its underbeak, as you will have seen it in zoos or in photographs.

The medieval heraldist and carver showed it with a long thin beak, like a heron's, and it is always drawn with its beak down, pecking at its breast. Its nest of young ones is often shown beneath it.

There is a reason why it is drawn like this. The artists of the Middle Ages rarely drew animals or birds from nature. They used the descriptions and illustrations which they found in books called "Bestiaries". These were collections of stories about the habits of animals, and were extremely popular with the monks and the few other people who could read.

Like the fables of Aesop, the Bestiaries used animals to teach moral or religious lessons. The pelican, for instance, is described as an unselfish bird. She pecks her breast and feeds her young with her own blood. Naturalists now know that she does nothing of the kind, but this is what she is doing on the shields and carvings where you may see her, and there are hundreds of them all over England.

The pelican of heraldry and art is usually called "the pelican in her piety", which means: "the pelican in her goodness or holiness".

The crane, a tall, long-legged bird like a heron, was drawn fairly accurately, but a curious story was told about her, as well. She is shown holding a lump of rock in her outstretched claw, and is called: "the crane in her *vigilance*", a word meaning "watchfulness". The Bestiary writers advised all good Christians to be on the watch for the devil, as the crane is on the watch for her enemies. She holds a rock in her claw so that if she should fall asleep, the rock would fall and wake her up.

The idea that the ostrich eats iron appears in the Bestiaries, and when the ostrich is used as a charge, it is shown with something like a horseshoe or key in its beak.

74. *A crane in her vigilance*

75. *An heraldic dolphin*

Like the animals and birds, the fish have their monarch. It is the dolphin, and is one of the finest of heraldic creatures, though, again, it is not drawn entirely as it appears in nature. It is extremely decorative, drawn in a bold S shape, with head down and tail up, a position called *embowed*. As you might expect, dolphins appear in the arms of families connected with naval history, and in those of some seaside towns and ports, such as Poole, Brighton and Devonport, in the south of England.

Several other kinds of fish are depicted in heraldry, but most of them are drawn rather alike, and it is difficult to tell what they are simply from their appearance. They are often used in canting arms. The eel appears in the Ellis arms; the roach in the Roche arms;

while the whale, a rare creature in heraldry, is used by the Whalleys, and by the Priory of Whalley in Lancashire, where three whales are drawn with bishops' croziers, or staffs, coming out of their mouths.

The pike, a large, fierce river fish, was known in heraldry as the "lucy". It appears in the arms of a powerful Norman family called de Luci. Because they married into many other noble families, the "lucy" can be found on a number of English shields. It is shown in picture 97 of the arms of the town of Erith, in Kent.

76. *The arms of Whalley Priory*

77. *The arms of Graham*

Snakes are used in heraldry, either tied in a figure of eight, or wound around a pillar or rod; tortoises, crabs, scorpions and snails all make their appearance in arms, while the scallop shell is one of the most frequently seen charges. The scallop was the emblem of St. James of Compostella, and many people used to go on pilgrimages to his shrine in Spain. Perhaps this explains the popularity of the shell in carvings and in heraldry.

Here is a shield with three escallops on the chief. It belongs to the Scottish family of Graham.

The insect most frequently to appear on shield and crest is the bee. It has always been an emblem of hard work, and often appears in the arms of towns which depend for their wealth upon industry. The bee is also used by several cities which begin with the letter B, such as Barrow-in-Furness, Blackburn, and Burnley. Bury, in Lancashire, has a bee for its crest.

78. *The crest of Bury, Lancashire*

Men and women do not often appear on shields, though they are sometimes found as supporters. Hands and arms, however, are fairly often used. A hand may be uncovered, or gloved, or in a steel gauntlet. The well-known arms of the Isle of Man show three legs in armour, bent at the knees, and joined at the thighs.

79. *The arms of the Isle of Man*

10. Monsters

Monsters and mythical creatures are so common in heraldry that many people think of them as "heraldic beasts". Not many of them, however, were invented by heraldists. Some are far older than the Middle Ages, and come from distant parts of the world. The dragon, for instance, is very ancient indeed and was known in Chinese art thousands of years ago.

The three most important monsters in heraldry are the wyvern, the dragon, and the griffin.

The *wyvern* has a scaly body, and wings of membrane, or skin, rather like a bat's. It has only two legs, and ends in a long tail, barbed at the end, curling or sometimes knotted. It is usually drawn in a "sejant" position, that is, sitting. Its head is dog-like, with a horn sticking out from the snout.

80. *A wyvern sejant*

45

81. *The arms of the City of London*

DOMINE NOS

DIRIGE

The *dragon* is not unlike the wyvern, but has *four* legs. Its feet are clawed, like an eagle's. Its large wings are similar to the wyvern's, and its tail is long and barbed.

The dragon was a Roman army emblem and came to Britain with the Roman legions. When the Roman army left, the dragon remained on the standards of the Britons who fought against the Anglo-Saxons. Eventually it became the emblem of Wales. The Welsh dragon appears as one of the supporters of the arms of Swansea on page 55.

The arms of the City of London are supported by a pair of dragons. The shield displays the red cross of St. George, and the sword of St. Paul, patron saint of the city and its cathedral.

The third monster, the *griffin*, or gryphon, you may remember from *Alice in Wonderland*. Like the dragon, it has four legs, but you can tell it apart from the other two by its feathered wings. Its hindquarters are those of a lion, and its head, though beaked and feathered, is adorned with the *ears* of a lion.

The shield of Cardinal Thomas Wolsey, one of Henry the Eighth's most powerful officials, is supported by two griffins. (See picture 82). In colour, the monsters' bodies are red and white, and their wings, beaks and legs are gold.

At the height of his power, Cardinal Wolsey planned to build a college at Oxford University, to be named after him, Cardinal College. In fact, it became Christ Church College, but it still uses Wolsey's armorial bearings, and these tell you a good deal about Wolsey himself.

Above his shield is his Cardinal's hat, and two kinds of cross used by important persons in the church. On the chief is a Tudor rose, a royal badge to signify his position as the king's minister. Wolsey had risen to his power in church and state from very humble origins, for he was the son of an Ipswich butcher. His arms contain two reminders of the county where he was born: the engrailed cross belonged to the Uffords, once the Earls of Suffolk, while the four leopards' faces came from the arms of the de la Pole family, the later Earls of Suffolk. The lion was the badge of Pope Leo X, who created Wolsey a Cardinal.

82. *The arms of Cardinal Wolsey*

The birds either side of the rose on the chief are Cornish choughs, and are taken from the arms of Wolsey's name-saint, St. Thomas à Becket. The chough was also known as a "becket", and is not uncommon in heraldry. It is a large black bird, with red legs and beak, and lives on rocky coasts, like those of Cornwall and Pembrokeshire. Though it is a rare bird nowadays, it was once far more numerous, and appears in several town and county arms, including Canterbury (of which Becket was Archbishop), Croydon, Wimbledon and Flintshire.

Dragons, wyverns and griffins are the most commonly used monsters, both on shields and crests, and as supporters. There are, however, a number of others. A beautiful and elegant creature, appearing in several town arms, is the *sea-horse*. Eastbourne and Margate both use one for a crest, and sea-horses support the arms of Ipswich, Newcastle-on-Tyne, and Cardiff, all of them sea-ports. They also support the shield of Cambridge, for the river Cam once brought sea-going ships to the university city.

Picture 83 shows the crest of Margate, in which the sea-horse holds a ship's mast.

83. *The crest of Margate, Kent*

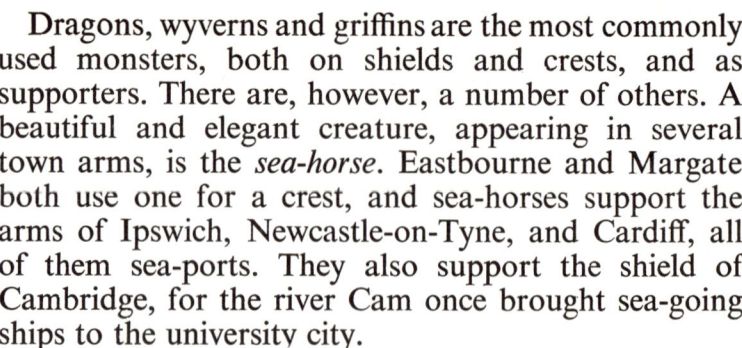

84. *An heraldic antelope*

85. *The phoenix*

Some monsters and legendary creatures were used most often as badges. The *heraldic antelope* was a badge of Henry the Fifth. It has horns with teeth like a pair of saws—the Bestiary writers said that it could cut down trees with them. The *phoenix* was one of Queen Elizabeth the First's many badges. It was a legendary bird, the only one of its kind. When it grew old, it built a fire of sweet-smelling wood, plunged into it and was reborn. It is therefore always shown "issuant from flames of fire". The *sea-lion* is the badge of the Port of London Authority, which also uses two sea-lions, holding banners, to support its shield. It is not the creature you see at the zoo, but simply a lion ending in a fish's tail. Its forefeet are usually webbed, like those of the sea-horse.

86. *The sea-lion*

The *pegasus*, or winged horse, was the badge of a medieval order of knights, the Templars, who, like

48

the Hospitallers (see page 35), played an important part in the Crusades. They pledged themselves to poverty, and there is a story that for economy two men shared the same horse. From a distance the two cloaked riders looked like wings, and this gave the Templars their Pegasus badge.

Two other heraldic monsters are the *cockatrice*, which is a wyvern with a cock's head, and the *mantygre*, which is a combination of lion, old man and goat.

87. *The winged horse or Pegasus*

The unicorn was one of the favourite beasts of medieval art and heraldry, and a creature of which many legends were told. It could only be captured with the help of a girl who must sit alone in a wood, while the hunters lay in wait, hidden. The unicorn would then lose its fear, come up to the girl and lay its head in her lap. The unicorn was thought to have immense strength and magic power. Its horn was believed to be a protection against poison. Pieces of so-called unicorn's horn were sold for enormous sums of money and much sought after. Queen Elizabeth the First possessed a valuable drinking cup of the horn. In fact, such things were what we should call today "fakes". The horns were really the tusks of the narwhal, or arctic whale, which were sometimes washed up on beaches.

88. *The cockatrice*

In heraldry the unicorn is best known as one of the supporters of the royal coat of arms. The Scottish royal arms have *two* as supporters, and you may remember that the title of one of the Scottish pursuivants is "Unicorn". Notice that the unicorn is not simply a horse with a horn. It has the divided hooves and the beard of a goat, while its tail is that of a lion.

89. *The mantygre*

90. *The unicorn*

11. What is it?

You would ask this question at once if you saw a shield with such odd-shaped charges upon it as those in picture 91. Yet these objects are not at all uncommon in heraldry. They are called *water-bougets*. A soldier of the Middle Ages would have known what they were without thinking. An army on the march had to have water, and one method of carrying it was in bags of skin. Pairs of these water-bags, suspended from a yoke, were laid across the backs of the baggage-animals. The word "bouget" is an old one, and a close relation of our word "bulge". A full skin must have bulged out on either side of a mule's round girth.

91. *The arms of Ross of Rosstrevor*

What about the three charges on the left?

92. *A maunch*

The first charge is called a *manche* or *maunch*, which means a sleeve. Ladies of the twelfth century wore sleeves with long flowing pieces of material dangling from the wrist. The sleeve was not sewn into the gown. It was worn separately, like a scarf, and was often of a different colour. It could be taken off and given to a knight to wear as a "favour" in his helmet, when he was jousting in a tournament.

93. *A fetterlock*

The second charge is a *fetterlock*. This has nothing to do with a horse's fetlock, though it sounds so similar. It represents a shackle and padlock, a kind of handcuff. Sometimes a falcon stands within it, as though it were his perch, and this device was adopted as a Yorkist badge in the Wars of the Roses.

94. *A pheon*

The barbed arrow head is called a *pheon*. The arms belong to the Sidney family. One of Queen Elizabeth the First's favourite young courtiers was the gifted poet and soldier, Sir Philip Sidney, who died of wounds, fighting against the Spaniards in the Netherlands. It was this Sidney who refused the water offered him and gave it to another soldier, with the words: "Thy need is greater than mine."

Among the sub-ordinaries on page 36 was a star-like charge called a *mullet*, which you remember is really the pricking part of a spur. The star of the sky is drawn rather differently, and is called an *estoile*. Its wavy rays are usually six in number. It appears on the shield of Sir Francis Drake, on either side of a wavy fess. These arms commemorate his voyage round the world in the *Golden Hind*.

95. *The arms of Drake*

The blazon for the shield would be: Sable, a fess wavy between two estoiles argent.

The curved side pieces on the shield in picture 96 are called *flaunches*, a word rather like our modern "flank". We talk of a horse's flank or the flanks of an army, meaning the sides. The field is *sable platy*, covered with the silver roundels known as *plates*.

The blazon for this shield would be: Sable platy, two flaunches argent.

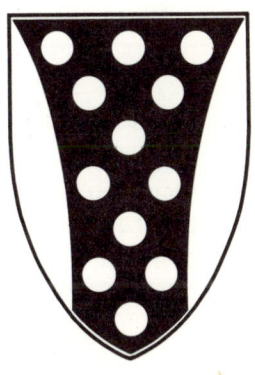

96. *The arms of Spelman*

Several other unusual charges can be found in the arms of this book. Do you remember, for instance, the caltraps of Stirlingshire? (Page 29).

Many of the objects you will see on a shield, however, are easily recognisable. There are devices connected with transport, such as wheels, stirrups and horse-shoes; innumerable charges connected with work and industry, such as barrels, knives, padlocks, keys and saws; arms of all kinds, from bows and arrows to cannons and hand grenades.

Very often, even if the arms are not actually canting ones, the charges have some connection with the family or town on whose shield or crest they appear. Some examples of this are given in the arms described in the next chapter. You would find it worth while looking for the arms of your own town and county, to see if the charges on them have a connection with it; perhaps a castle; or a wavy fess to signify a river; a bridge or a windmill; or some device representing a local industry, either of today or from its earlier history.

12. Town and Country

97. The arms of Erith

Here are the old arms of Erith, a large town in Kent which has now become part of the London Borough of Bexley. In the new borough arms, the white horse shown here is included in the crest. The blazon is easy to understand: Argent, a fleur-de-lys sable between three lucies (pike-fish) gules; on a canton gules a horse rampant argent.

The armorial bearings used by local authorities are known as "civic" arms, and most of them have only been granted officially by the College of Arms in the last hundred years. The devices on them are, however, often very old indeed and are not there just by chance.

Since the twelfth century, city corporations have used seals on their documents, and, to prevent forgery, these seals were engraved with elaborate devices. Later, when towns became important, the corporations adopted coats of arms, and frequently transferred to their shields the devices already used on their town seals. These charges may be borrowed from the arms of a local family; they may be connected with the history of the district, or portray some landmark, such as a castle, or river, or bridge. Very often they contain a reference to agriculture or industry.

The lucies, or pike-fish, in the arms of Erith are a pun on the name of de Luci, a medieval family who owned much land in Kent. The fleur-de-lys has always been widely used. Its connection with royal heraldry has already been explained. The white horse on the red canton, or square, is the oldest charge on the shield and has an interesting history.

Well over a thousand years ago, in the fifth and sixth centuries, England was invaded by hordes of fierce, plundering tribes from the north of what is now called Germany. They were the Angles, Saxons and Jutes. Kent was overrun and successfully occupied by the Jutes under the leadership of their kings, Hengist and Horsa. Whether men of these names actually existed is not at all certain. The word Hengist means a stallion, and Horsa a mare, and it was believed that the Jutes carried banners, displaying a white horse on a red field. Kent adopted the device on the county arms and it appears in the arms of several Kentish towns.

52

The German invaders who gave their emblem of a white horse to Kent, left their mark on other county arms. Picture 98 shows the shield of the county of Essex.

98. The arms of Essex

In the Middle Ages, it was believed that the Anglo-Saxons fought with broad, notched swords. Essex and Middlesex, once the ancient kingdoms of the East and Middle Saxons, each have these swords on their shields. They are called *seaxes*. The Middlesex shield differs from that of Essex in having a crown above the seaxes. It is of a special type called a Saxon crown, a gold circlet with three tall points, each ending in a ball. Both shields are red, and the seaxes silver with gold hilts.

99. A Saxon crown

100. The crest of Sheffield

Sheffield in Yorkshire uses on its shield the same arrows that appear in the crest on the left, a symbol of the steel trade for which Sheffield has long been famous. The lion belongs to the Earls of Shrewsbury who held the manor when Sheffield was only a village.

Wallasey is in Cheshire. You may recognise the "garbs" or wheatsheaves which the Cheshire family of Grosvenor adopted as armorial bearings after the dispute with Lord Scrope (see page 16). The three-masted ship on the sea stands for the shipping and sea-trading interests of the city.

The story behind the bugle-horn is not so obvious. Near Wallasey is a part of Cheshire known as the Wirral. It was once a forest owned by the Earls of Chester, who employed a Master Forester to look after it. He, of course, used a horn when organising hunting parties for the Earl and his household. The Stanley family were Master Foresters at one time when the Wirral really was a forest, and they still have a "Wirral horn" in their possession. The district is now largely built over, but the bugle-horn in Wallasey's arms is a reminder of the days when the port was on the edge of a forest.

101. The arms of Wallasey

You may know Wolverhampton as a modern industrial city in the heart of the Black Country. It is only in recent times, however, that it has developed from a village into a city, and its coat of arms contains charges that go back to very early times.

102. *The arms of Wolverhampton*

The large cross in the centre is thought to have been adopted in memory of a Saxon Christian called Wulfrun, who founded a religious house at the small village of Hamton. The place became known as "Wulfrun's Hamton", and this came to be pronounced "Wolverhampton."

The four other charges on the shield all have some connection with local history. The pillar represents a Saxon fragment still standing in St. Peter's Church. The book represents the grammar school. The woolsack records Wolverhampton's wealth as a small medieval town, when the wool trade made it prosperous. The padlock is a reminder that in the eighteenth century the city's locksmiths were said to be the finest in England.

The crest shows the crossed keys of St. Peter, patron saint of the church, while the black beacon and the motto both refer to the local coal and ironstone mining industries.

Here therefore, is an achievement whose charges range over more than a thousand years of history, from Saxon to modern times.

Picture 103 shows the arms of Swansea. Swansea is a great modern sea-port in Wales, and the wavy lines at the base of the shield, in blue and white, obviously refer to this. The arms were only granted in 1922, but the osprey and fish have been used by the city for hundreds of years. The town was granted the right to use them in 1306 by William de Braose, Lord of Gower.

The lion is also from the de Braose arms, and the castle around which the city grew up was in the possession of that family. The same de Braose lion supports one side of the shield, while the other supporter is the red Welsh dragon. Both animals are "gorged", that is, they wear coronets around their necks.

Arms have been granted to universities, and schools, and to bodies like the City of London Livery Companies. Arms of this type, and those of towns and counties, are known as "corporate arms" because they belong to a body of people (*corpus* is the Latin for "body"), not to a single person.

The arms of one of Britain's new universities, that of Sussex, appears on the colour page opposite page 12. Most of the charges have been chosen for their connection with Sussex and south-east England. The *two dolphins* of the crest are taken from the shield of Brighton, outside which the University is situated. The *six gold martlets* belong both to Brighton's arms and to those of the West Sussex County Council, while the *Saxon crowns* are reminders of King Harold's death at Hastings. The supporters are "pelicans in their piety" (see page 42), shown here standing upon books to signify learning. They are unusual in that each holds a banner. The *stag's head* of the sinister banner comes from the arms of Eastbourne, which has *two stags' heads argent on a fess gules*. The dexter banner carries the *demi-lion conjoined to the hulk of a ship* that belongs to the arms of the Cinque ports, towns in Sussex and Kent which provided ships for the king's navy in the Middle Ages.

103. *The arms of Swansea*

13. Becoming a Heraldry Collector

104. *The impaled arms of husband and wife*

You do not have to live in an old cathedral city or an historic town with a castle, to find interesting examples of heraldry. Even newly built "satellite towns" and modern housing estates will have coats of arms on such buildings as banks and schools, and upon local authority notice-boards and vehicles.

You may also find examples of heraldry in churches. Even if you live in what seems to be a very modern town, it has probably grown up around an old one, and its parish church may be a medieval building. This is true of many of the suburbs of London and other large cities. The church will contain tombs and wall tablets and some of them are sure to have carved and painted achievements. Here you will probably see a shield something like the one in picture 104, which appears to be two shields in one. This, in fact, is just what it is. These "two-in-one" coats of arms are used for married couples and often appear on their tombs.

The shield above shows the imaginary arms of a Sir John Talbot and his wife, Lady Isabella. Her name before she married was Grey. The husband's arms are placed on the dexter side of the shield, and the wife's on the sinister. If you have forgotten what this means, it is explained on page 33. Sir John Talbot has a canting coat of arms: a talbot or foxhound. Lady Isabella's family have: argent, a bend sable.

When the shield is divided like this to show the two coats of arms belonging to the families of a husband and wife, it is called *impaled*, because the shield is divided down the centre by a *pale*.

Usually, the children of the marriage inherit only their father's arms. The young Talbots would, therefore, use only the foxhound on their shield. There is, however, a case when children inherit their mother's arms as well as their father's. Suppose that Isabella Grey's father had died, and that she had no brothers. She then inherited her family estates and arms. If her children had used *only* the Talbot foxhound, the Grey arms would have died out. To prevent this, the children "quartered" the arms of Talbot and Grey, as shown in picture 105.

56

These became the Talbot arms of the younger generation. If one of the sons married a lady whose arms were already quartered in this way, their marriage shield would show *eight* divisions. (See picture 106.) Indeed, in some cases the number of quarterings multiplied so much that it became impossible to show them all. There are families whose quarterings run into over a hundred, and could only be shown clearly on an out-sized shield. It is usual today to keep a record of them, and use a simpler coat of arms, showing the chief armorial bearings of the family.

105. *The quartered arms of Talbot and Grey*

106. *Shield with eight divisions*

You will sometimes see arms displayed not on a shield, but on a shape like a diamond. This is called a *lozenge*, and women use it because, of course, they would never have carried a shield. Many tombs show the arms of the husband on one side on a shield, the wife's arms on the other on a lozenge, and in the centre the impaled marriage arms, like the ones in picture 104.

Only the eldest son inherited the family title and estates; the family arms also passed to him when his father died. Till then, he wore them "differenced". The eldest son's mark of difference was some kind of "label", a strip across the chief with three or more points hanging from it. The commonest type of label is that shown here, but you will find labels with more points, and sometimes with charges, such as ermine spots, upon them.

107. *The eldest son's label for difference. The Black Prince is shown wearing this on page 26*

The second son used a crescent, the third a mullet, the fourth a martlet (swallow). There were marks of difference right down to the ninth son. These small devices remained permanently on the arms of these younger members of the family.

Heraldry can be seen on monuments and in stained glass in even the smallest village churches, but it is, of course, the great cathedrals and abbeys which have the richest heraldry. Canterbury Cathedral, for instance, has some fine shields and badges, especially those on the stone gateway leading to the cathedral. Here the Tudor portcullis and rose can be seen, and, in the centre, the Tudor royal arms, supported by a dragon and a greyhound. This shield is divided into four quarters, two displaying the lions of England, and two the French fleurs-de-lys. These are the arms shown on the herald's tabard on page 23.

108. *The arms of Richard the Lionheart*

Royal heraldry has changed a good deal at different periods, as you will notice if you keep a look-out for the carved and painted royal arms which you sometimes see hanging on church walls, and which appear on the signboards of hotels called the King's Arms or the Royal Arms.

The lion can be traced back to the time of Henry First, in the early twelfth century. He used a lion as a badge. His daughter, Maud, married Geoffrey Planta-genet, and Henry granted his son-in-law a blue shield, covered with small gold lions. These, however, were rampant, not passant as they are today. It was Richard the Lionheart (1189–1199) who first used three gold lions passant guardant on a red field, arms which remained the same through the reigns of John, Henry the Third, and Edward the First and Second.

109. *The arms of Edward III*

In 1340 Edward the Third divided his shield into four quarters.

In I and IV, the most important quarters, he placed the royal fleurs-de-lys of France, of which he claimed to be king through his mother, Isabella, daughter of Philip the Fourth of France.

In II and III he placed the lions of England. These arms can be seen on his tomb in Westminster Abbey. The fleurs-de-lys were later reduced to three in number, and continued to appear on the royal arms until the death of Queen Elizabeth in 1603.

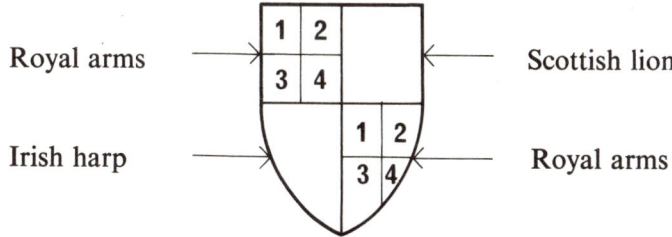

Royal arms — Scottish lion

Irish harp — Royal arms

110. *The quartered arms of the Stuarts*

111. *The Irish harp*

The Stuart kings, who ruled from 1603 to 1688, except during the period of the Commonwealth, placed the old royal arms into the first and fourth quarters. The Irish harp now appears for the first time in the third quarter, and the arms of Scotland in the second.

The Scottish arms consist of a gold field, on which is a red lion rampant, with blue tongue and claws. The lion stands within a narrow double border of red, called a *double tressure flory counter-flory*. This rather complicated name means that the double tressure is decorated with fleurs-de-lys, their heads alternately inwards and outwards. Only the top and bottom of each fleur-de-lys can be seen.

112. *The arms of Scotland*

Between 1688 and the beginning of Queen Victoria's reign in 1837, the royal arms changed more than once, to incorporate the arms of the House of Orange (William the Third) and of the House of Hanover (the four Georges). In 1837, the royal arms took their present form, with the lions in quarters I and IV, the Scottish arms in II, and the Irish harp in III.

Ever since the Middle Ages, craftsmen have found in heraldry a fine subject for their skill in wood and stone carving, in stained glass, and in brass-engraving. It is not only in church buildings that you can see examples of their work. Many castles and great houses now open to the public have heraldic ceilings, fireplaces and windows, and coats of arms above their gates and over their porches.

Today, many counties display their arms on boards set up at the side of major roads, as you enter the county. Many towns, too, illustrate their arms, often with a list of the interesting buildings to be found in the city. The modern interest in heraldry is also shown by the metal plaques of county arms which people fix to the back of their cars.

It is worth while keeping your eyes open for heraldic postcards, postage stamps, letter-headings and wine-labels. Great Britain had a set of armorial stamps for the Festival of Britain in 1951, consisting of half-crown, five shillings and one pound stamps. Most European countries have issued heraldic stamps at some time, and some foreign cities have postcards showing their arms. Perhaps the finest stamps were those issued in France some years ago, showing the arms of the different Departments, or districts, and those of her colonies.

To make a collection of armorial stamps would, perhaps, be difficult and expensive, but to keep a "heraldry book" is within the reach of anyone really interested in the subject. If you use a large loose-leaf book, you can paste into it anything you find: stamps, postcards, wine labels, letterheadings, pictures cut from magazines and newspapers.

If you have a camera, you will find that shields and achievements photograph extremely well, especially in colour. Flash equipment is easy to use (though expensive unfortunately) and it enables you to take examples of heraldry in churches, not only on tombs, but in stained glass windows, provided, of course, that the shields are not too high up. You need plenty of sunlight behind the window for this, otherwise the colours hardly show.

Heraldry is a large subject, and much has had to be left out of this short book. I have tried to tell you about the place of heraldry in history; what you can learn from a shield about the family or corporation which uses it; and how many devices belonged to a common stock of knowledge and legend which not only heraldists but other medieval artists were very familiar with, and used in their arts.

If you want to find out more about the subject, there is a list of heraldry books which may be in your public library, on page 63. If they are not, the librarian would get them for you.

113. *An heraldic stamp*

SHORT GLOSSARY OF HERALDIC TERMS

Some of these words have page references because there is more about them in the book. Words with no page references are extra heraldic terms which you might want to know. Those with a star after them are illustrated here.

At gaze

ACHIEVEMENT	complete display of armorial bearings *pp.* 7, 8 and 24
ADDORSED	figures or objects placed back to back, like the dolphins in the crest of Sussex University, opposite *p.* 12
ANNULET	a ring; one of the sub-ordinaries *p.* 36
AT GAZE*	term for a standing deer; AT SPEED a running deer *p.* 40
ATTIRES*	stag's antlers; the points are TINES *p.* 40
BEZANT	gold roundel; BEZANTY strewn with bezants *p.* 37
BILLET	small oblong charge; BILLETY strewn with billets *p.* 36
BLAZON	the language of heraldry *p.* 8
BORDURE	border round the edge of the shield *p.* 36
CADENCY MARKS	small charges used by sons to DIFFERENCE their arms from their father's. See LABEL, CRESCENT and MULLET
CANTING ARMS	punning arms *pp.* 7, 8
CANTON	small square in dexter chief of shield *pp.* 36, 52
CHAPEAU*	ermine lined cap *p.* 29
CHARGE	any object placed on a shield *pp.* 8, 33
CINQUEFOIL*	rose-like flower of five petals
COMPARTMENT	mound, usually of grass, set below the shield; the supporters stand on it *p.* 55
COMPONY*	border or ordinary divided into alternate metal and tincture squares; also called GOBONY
COUNTERCHANGED*	a charge of two colours on a field of the same two, with the colours reversed *p.* 23
COUPED*	a branch, stalk or limb cut clean across
CRESCENT*	moon with points upwards; used in CADENCY to denote second son
DIFFERENCE	see CADENCY MARKS
ERASED*	torn off, leaving ragged points
ESCUTCHEON	another word for shield, always used when a small shield appears as a charge

Attires

Chapeau

Cinquefoil

Compony or gobony

Counterchanged

Crescent

Couped

Erased

ESTOILE	star, usually with six straight and six wavy points *p.* 51	
FETTERLOCK*	form of padlock, or handcuff *p.* 50	Fetterlock
FIELD	background colour or fur used on shield *p.* 8	
FIMBRIATED*	used of a charge with narrow border of different colour	
FITCHÉ*	term used of cross with pointed foot	Fimbriated
FLAUNCHE	pair of curved lines each side of shield *p.* 51	
FRET	design of interlacing strips *pp.* 36, 37	
FUSIL	elongated diamond shape; one of the sub-ordinaries *pf.* 23, 36	
GARB	heraldic term for wheatsheaf *pp.* 16, 53	Fitché
GORGED	encircled round neck, usually with collar, chain or coronet *pp.* 12, 40, 54	
GOUTTÉ	covered with drops *p.* 38	
GYRON	triangular charge in dexter chief; GYRONY* shield divided from centre point into GYRONS	Gyrony
IMPALED*	shield divided down centre, with husband's arms on dexter and wife's on sinister; archbishops, bishops, Kings of Arms and certain others may IMPALE their own arms with the arms of the office they hold *p.* 56	Impaled
LABEL	bar with "points", usually three, four or five, used by eldest son during his father's lifetime *p.* 57	
LOZENGE	diamond-shaped charge; also used instead of shield to display a woman's arms *p.* 57	Maunch
MANTLING	streamers of cloth, usually in two colours, coming from base of helmet and spread out on either side of shield *pp.* 26, 27	
MARSHALLING	science of showing marriage alliances on a shield *p.* 56	
MARTLET	heraldic swallow, usually drawn without feet *pp.* 42, 57	Mill-rind
MAUNCH*	lady's sleeve used as a charge *p.* 50	
MILL-RIND*	iron band in centre of millstone	
MULLET or MOLET	five-pointed star, really pricking part of a spur; also used in CADENCY to denote third son *p.* 36; mullet of six points *p.* 30	Orle
ORDINARIES	charges of geometrical type such as bend, pale, fess, chief *p.* 33	
ORLE*	border composed of small charges	
PHEON*	broad arrow-head, with engrailed inner edges *p.* 50	Pheon

62

PIERCED	with a round hole in the middle. Mullets and other small objects are often pierced *p. 29*	Pile
PILE*	wedge-shaped charge (an ordinary)	
POTENT*	field composed of T-shaped patterns	
PROPER	anything in its natural colour, such as a hand	Potent
RAMPANT*	position of lion, and some other animals, upright on hind feet *p. 39*	
ROUNDELS	small circular charges, in different colours *pp. 36, 37*	
SALTIRE	diagonal cross *p. 33*	Rampant
SEAX*	Saxon broad-sword, with notch *p. 53*	
SEMÉ	field or charge strewn with small objects, such as billets, drops, roses *p. 38*	Seaxes
STOCK	tree-stump; also the shaft of an anchor	
SUPPORTERS	figures holding up shield on either side *pp. 27, 28*	
TREFOIL*	shamrock leaf, with three lobes	
VAIR	alternating pattern of blue and white, representing squirrel's fur *p. 31*	Trefoil
WATER-BOUGET	charge taken from leather water-panniers *p. 50*	

MORE BOOKS TO READ

SIMPLE HERALDRY by Iain Moncreiffe and Don Pottinger (Nelson); a short and clear outline of heraldry with amusing illustrations.

BOUTELL'S HERALDRY revised by C. W. Scott-Giles and J. P. Brooke-Little (Warne); an essential reference book, in which the information is clearly set out and generously illustrated.

SHIELD AND CREST by Julian Franklyn (MacGibbon and Kee); particularly valuable for its fine illustrations, many of which are coloured.

THE ROMANCE OF HERALDRY by C. W. Scott-Giles (Dent); an enjoyable book, linking heraldry with Britain's history and literature.

CIVIC HERALDRY OF ENGLAND AND WALES by C. W. Scott-Giles (Dent); this gives full descriptions and black and white illustrations of town and county arms.

BOOK OF FLAGS by G. Campbell and I. O. Evans (Oxford).

In addition to these general works there are many which are of more specialised interest. Canterbury Cathedral and Westminster Abbey both publish their own booklets on their heraldry; the arms of the Guilds of the City of London, of Oxford and Cambridge Universities, are dealt with fully in special books; so is the heraldry of Scotland, and such branches of the subject as heralds and church heraldry. Your public library will probably possess a variety of heraldry books, or would obtain some for you.

INDEX

Terms already explained in the glossary are omitted from the index, except for a few important words. The numbers refer to pages in the book. The letter *f.* after a number means "and on the following pages".